Head on a Pike

david v. d'andrea

Matt Pike

Head on a Pike

The Illustrated Lyrics of Matt Pike

with alyssa maucere

RARE BIRD

THIS IS A GENUINE RARE BIRD BOOK

Rare Bird Books
453 South Spring Street, Suite 302
Los Angeles, CA 90013
rarebirdlit.com

Rare Bird Books Subsidiary Rights Department
453 South Spring Street, Suite 302
Los Angeles, CA 90013

Set in Dante
Printed in the United States

10 9 8 7 6 5 4 3 2 1

Publisher's Cataloging-in-Publication Data available upon request.

This book is dedicated to London Agnes

david b. d'andrea

Contents

I

Art of
Self Defense

artwork by

Santos

Bagdad

Quickening of the Elder
Knowledge of the Other side
Deep weed sets emotion
Hardening of the Warrior
The burning
That will never die
Melding of the Riffchild
From wall to the Universe
Weed priest stoned arrival
Sharpening of the weapons
The skill inside the endless mind

Celestial King walks water
Hear words foretell destruction
Hear words expose corruption
Generation darkening

Echoes from the mountain
A warning to behold the times
Insight saved the blind man
Covenant with the Father
The burning that will never die
Supersonic psalmist project
Reveals astro-child
Windows of the Riffian
Nameless masses cower
From horse and carriage
In the sky

10,000 Years

10,000 years or more
In jet black meditation
Sonic Temptress hears no more
And hands me my salvation
Walking thru the piles of life
Ignore all accusation
Now I stand here hands are sore
But that's my motivation

The vision never died
The earthling walked in flight
10,000 Years or more
In jet black meditation
Now I stand here hands are sore
But that's my reputation

Blood from Zion

Flies Cloudian Rider
Holding keys to fires
A righteous one begat him
His robe is drenched in blood

Fury is beside him
Knees before The Master
Righteous praise from Zion
Wicked born fire

Coming of Messiah
Hand of the Almighty
Blood flows down from Zion
Turn face from the Cherubim.

Last

And you crawled in the room with the serpent
And they sucked from your body the poison
Then the Cyclops arrived there to warn you
And the Whore entered in to adore you
Seems like life has dawned to fade away

Ice bards' ship the frozen bodies
And the ones in the Son are immortal
Then the skeleton hands you the needle
You were born to this day from the cradle
Seems like life dawned to fade away

Reaper's scythe harvest time is upon you
No more use for abuse in this body
Father Time gives the wings now to free you
In the coffin your destiny's beat you

Fireface

To be rising chief I have traveled a hundred fold days
Wandered dark wilderness, ravens have gathered my ways
Holy man, vision quest, dancing dawn reflects his gaze
Return to the clan with the scalps of the men who betrayed

Medicine Man has concocted a potion to see
Animal Spirits have filled me and leads what's to be
Running wolf, eagle eyes, blood running cold in my veins
Great Spirit laughs as my enemies run from my reign

To be rising chief I have traveled a hundred fold days
Wandered dark wilderness ravens have gathered my ways
Look in my eyes your demise is what is fueling my rage
For I am the one whom by others is called Fire Face

Master of Fists

Anger flows, warriors call
Focused eyes see thru them all
Teacher's death was a con
Jeet Kune Do avenging one

Streamline form, flying kicks
Warriors fall from powered hits
Mesmerized speed and fury
Nunchaku crush skulls with their flurry

Snap of the dragon
Crack like a whip
You cannot defy
The Master of Fists

Bender of will
Defender of bliss
Enters the dragon
The Master of Fists

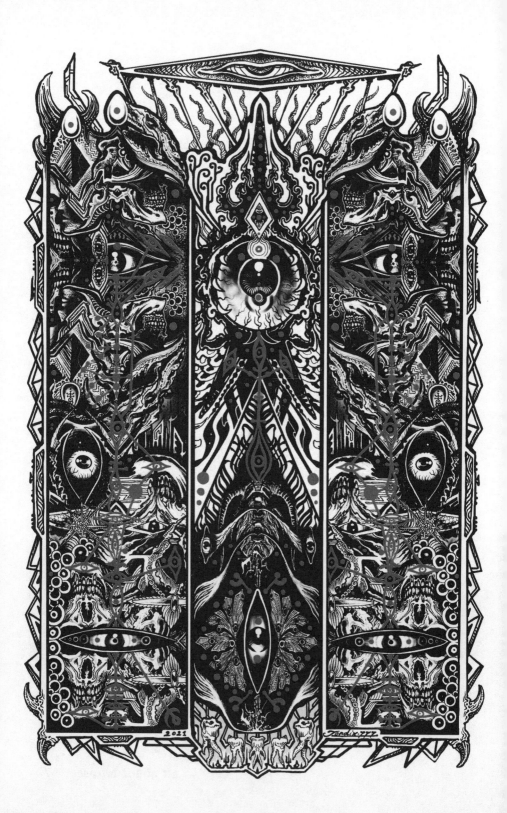

II

Surrounded by Thieves

artwork by

Jondix

Eyes and Teeth

Now you are lost and can't find
Gazes the teeth and white eyes
Lost all your reason, insanity
Nowhere to run, could this be

Chills up your neck, down your spine
Now you must run for your life
Monsters prevail, insanity
Nowhere has swallowed your being

Run from the blackness of night
Evil has you in its sight
Adrenaline madness won't let you be
No one could hear your last screams

Hung, Drawn and Quartered

The candle has burnt through,
The wax that once covered my eyes
The Pharisees told you,
But you knew of the black serpent lies
Come all ye losers, don't you know you're the children of life
Follow me now and we'll burn down the pillars of time

The evil has come and the darkness will cover the light
Above the legions, who will slay the poor and the blind
Warriors that follow,
Won't you read the sign and the time
Stand now in battle and we'll crush the clan and their kind

Speedwolf

Befriend a bastard, a thief as your brother
Heard him say what's yours is mine
Careful when gouging yourself with what's holy
I see through your transparent lies

Skeleton symphonies play psalms to tell you
Your venom has blinded your eyes
Make sure your rope is real strong when you hang me
Better make sure that I die

Your name became Judas the moment I helped you
Should've just let it all lie
If Mammon's the reason for killing your hero
Choke on your evil disguise

The
Yeti

Beyond the mountains of ice
Exists a creature of frost
His secret lies in the skies
Eternal legend survives
His powers unknown by man
To catch a glimpse if he can
Wandering deep polar caps
Communication with saucer
Abominable nomad
The ancient monks know his clan
The time of yeti will rise
Because his ways have been wise
The yeti's feet take flight,
Upon the tundran ice
Carries the saucer's key,
Upon the space bound seed
The yeti's feet take flight,
Upon the tundran ice
Carries the saucer's key,
Upon the space bound seed

Nemesis

Come, enter the feast, eat flesh of kings
Hands crying blood, scourge making way
Sonic its sound, destroyer comes down
Feet plant on earth, forcing the toll
Wasting what was, reap what you sow
Hammer of death delivers the blow

Invincible throne, tormenting hate
Eyes of the God, sombering souls
Dark is the cape, a dissident's face
Holy the war, laying in wait
Lashes that burn, crucified mass
Looked for the light, but death betrays

Devil's hooked tongue, black takes away
Ashes arise, clouds of their faith
Hatred becomes the infidel's graves
Unveil thy cloak, forge the mine curse
Demon seed womb, dictator's birth
Come to conspire control of the earth

Thraft of Canaan

Ocean quest upon me, shoreline fades away
The mighty men drifting night and day
The sea has tossed them, beast beheld their eyes
Ready the ships, now it's do or die

Forged of blackened steel, wields the iron hand
Voices loud as thunder, pillaging the land
Drone seeks mortal vision, pulse the silver steed
Riding out to conquer all humanity

I'm high on fire, heads are searing
Give with pain all thy hearing
Promised land never veering
I'm stoned again, reset bearing

Surrounded by Thieves

Icy caverns
Holds man traveler
Ancient relic
Reveals secrets

Transform human
Beyond mortal
Learnt foreboding
Sacred tempest

Up to their bridles in blood
The wars of the Earth have begun
The sunless age comes so it seems
The cities surrounded by thieves

Rich man he lusts for gold
Still there are slaves to be sold
Woe to the one who had saved
The cities surrounded by graves

Razor Hoof

Razor hoof coming down
Coming down, coming down
Antlers sharp, sharp to kill
Trampler unseen
Fearless wolf, bring it on
Bring it down, bring it down
Weeks without
Kills for blood

Corpse wolf, now raised

III

Blessed Black Wings

artwork by

Brian Mercer

Devilution

Man's done, Babylon, eat the fruit divine, wasted labyrinth
Snake's tongue, lies sung, master of disguise, poison conqueror
War torn, plague born, live in ancient wrath, executioner
Shape shift, lives sift, pain in the child's eyes,
last rite spoken - Devilution

Web spun, death comes, bring the blackened tide,
rising war god
Blood lit planet awakes the lurking time,
raging maelstrom
Arcane macabre deity arrives
spewing hellfire
Twisted acrid abominating guise,
promised vengeance - Devilution

Dark king suffering, know the elder's toll, deceiving millions
Men hung, pain comes, worship me or die, as you lie broken
End all wars call, stand your ground and try, hopeless victim
Man's done, Babylon, eat the fruit divine,
wasted labyrinth - Devilution

The Face of Oblivion

Ghosts of forever ride the pale twilight
Teller of the tale lives beneath the ice
Shadow of the haunter creeps within our sight
As we lay sleeping... Horror

Shunned dead city in the acrid cold
Thawed out the specimens as the blood unfolds
Blasts uncover terrors that shouldn't be
Elder race lives... Arkham

Expedition through the Titan Mountains
Sepulcher unveils beings arcane
Things uncovered make the men insane
Embrace our madness

The blood I shed for you was divine
So turn you head and leave it denied
I call your name in the cold of the night
Now you've become the serpent's spine

Brothers in the Wind

The lot is cast mysteries vast
alive your eyes as conscience dies
As he runs he's taken from the world
we know the dealer's blow
Embrace our faith without a trace
wonder takes our earthly days
Not forgot just left behind
the prison will not always bind

And if the sun never shined on us
the night time has fruit of the vine
Come with me now and just lie to me
tonight we'll pretend we're alive
Our brother's wind flows on and on...

Bones and flesh lives that rest
holy blood the spirit's quest
Beauty ties the end's disguise
a somber dirge cause angels die
A sky of gray the coffins lay
the sun will come another day
Not forgot just left behind
the prison will not always bind

Where have I wandered my father
led like lamb to my slaughter
Truth has awakened the dreamer
hand I the keys to the keeper

Cometh Down Hessian

Enter stoned paravex
Mother of the Seekers
Cometh down hessian
to plunder the archaic tomb

Stolen ancient amulet
Black the hexed sarcophagus
Summoning the hound
the bringer of impending doom

Necromatic lunatics
murder of the innocents
Stepping on the curse
Inflicting it's bestial wounds
Undo the evil spell
Undig the graves demise
Unveiling the horror
The hair covered corpse now will lie

Blessed Black Wings

Long to live the path that saves my soul
Away adapted forced to live so low
Gone's the will to want to see the light
Somber visions cause the path I've strived
Sooth The Sayer revels in my death
Some would think I'm just a lunatic
The blood I bleed must be black indeed
Speak the devil in my time of need

Blessed black wings

Subterranean the house of worms
Enter in and let my voice be heard
They call to me bearing evil grins
Accounting all here is the den of sins

Blessed black wings

Pleasure's treasures leave me hypnotized
Blacking out, follow the trail of lies
Demons seen with a knife in back
Eat your mouth out with your cocaine slack
Shadow powder makes me come alive
Walking zombie mumbles depressed sighs
The blood I bleed must be black indeed
Speak the devil in my time of need

Blessed black wings

Anointing of Seer

Onward the seer,
Glass ships of fear,
Marauder's path
Gaze in her eyes,
Sacred and wise,
Prophecy
Lost in her trance,
In her eyes the flames dance,
Foreboding
Truth of her days,
Black endless rays,
Shows the Skyr

Damsel in chains,
For love the bard reigns,
Destroyer
Skills surpass strength,
Towers that quake,
Song of doom
Unsinkable stars,
Bring powers at large,
The day they mote
The shaking of Teir,
Sonic psalm terrors,
Chains are freed

Come to me champion
Your life has been sieged in me
Calling from distances
Yearning to be set free

To Cross the Bridge

Wandering warlord, tales of horror
Quest and saga snares the batterer
Fallen victim taken capture, wheel of pain
Gives strength to un-mastered

Chained and shackled, earthen toil
Made to serve the whips and lashes
Quench your thirst and drink this bottle
The warrior's chains are self inflicted

Lay the steps upon the mountain
Open gates reveal the temple
Quench your thirst and drink this bottle
The warrior's chains are self inflicted

Mirrored armor reflects squalor
A day will come when I will conquer
Take your stand and cross my line
The eye Aleph has seen my kind

Silver Back

Drive the fist into your face, and blacken your eye
Unearthly sounds rumble guts, and stomp your insides
Riffs have come, your fate is sung, don't even try
Blacks the set, kills all the rest, the slay masters fly

Enter in the battle ground, you've come to my time
Black arena, till the death, a game we play blind
You've stepped your bounds, beg for life, if we'd be so kind
Drive the fist into your face and blacken your eyes

IV

Death is this Communion

artwork by

Skinner

Fury Whip

Slit throat holocaust,
Dark's the day of Pentecost
Waiting for the ships to turn the tide
Black fiend, treachery, the numbers fall, you wear thirteen
Pray the demons cannot kill the light
Killed dead, splitting head, making sure the lion's fed
Hanging by a thread that holds your life
Pain King, suffering; walk on through the acid ring
Imprisoned but your hands are still untied
The fool's religion
Unprophet's truth
Live self destruction
Bad luck's your noose
Sin, sex, bad intent, making sure the money's spent
Watching as your dollars turn to dimes
Death tax, broken backs, 'time has come to wield the axe
Paying for the check and all your crime

Waste of Tiamat

Twisting, falling, like eagles they drop from the sky
Without warning, the nuclear beast shows its eyes
Chaos ramped, the cult of the severed head rise
Among the ashes, could not foresee strength or size

Haunting screaming, gone in a flash of our eyes
Priestly being meant nothing more than their guise
Fallen angels, light up the sky with demise
Blackened hydra makes way as dark men conspire

Demons swarming, attacking the few who survive
Armageddon, the heavens and hell will collide
Cometh conqueror, black death is allotted its time
Primly power, to walk through the blood is divine

Death is this Communion

The site of the lost horizons, the minion seek to resurrect a God
The graves hold arcane mysteries, various swamps hide terrible catacombs
The circle of redeemers, the pact is made with human sacrifice
Under storm filled skies, behemoth of the sea awakes...arise

Tremble at the horror in which it writhes
Once they behold and unearth the titans might
Faithful servants pay its ghastly price
Slithering, blasphemous, curse upon all life

Now you realize
Death is this communion

Turk

I cannot grasp this black psychology
My cage's walls are closing in on me
The rage that surfaces is not my soul
It's like a devil taking control
The violence lives in me ad will not leave
Live a magician with pain up his sleeve
The sight of God is to unfold
Memories untold
For every poem's a rhyme
The joke is father time

Our delves in twisted sexuality
Substance abuse and immortality
A stark obsession no one else would know
Questions unanswered, how far can this go
The wall of torment, my blood's boiling
Break this shell to do what's so obscene

Rumors of War

Howling tracks of Hell track coming,
Black storm on the rise
They fill out temples with their lies

The snakes come slithering
Anarchy
Chaotic hunters rise
Spit in their evil eyes

Stand our ground with hate and fury;
Fear that comes will die
Our enemies have come to life

Now they exalt the fiend
Shotgun
Your nightmare's not a dream
They'll choke you and your screams

All comes clashing
The haunting presence controlling all that breaths
It's brought the world down to it knees

The hounds of hell are freed
Desolate
And with their bite, disease
His evil never sleeps

Sacrificing sons and daughters, rolls the war machine
The tyrant fills his destiny

The snakes come slithering
Anarchy
Chaotic hunters rise
Spit in the evil eyes

Cyclopian Scape

Reptile race crossbred down through the golden age, human haze
Lemurian throne taken and usurped by the alien drones, controlled and honed
Atlantian keys sunken and destroyed by catastrophe, left wandering
Bloodline kings slither down through society's reptoid disease
Cataclysm to the elder tribes
Aununnaki have survived
Continents underwater shrine
Ocean vaults holding time
Say ye grace unto the serpent line
Unviel curses and their lies
Contemplate the lengths they'll go to rule
As their fangs dig into you

Ethereal

The skill and mind of magic
Holding the mystic doors
Like moths of ancient light
Follow ascend in flight
Fall through the ether lakes
Gliding through daemon halls
It's black wings wrap around me
Fires glow red and white
A metamorphosis
Until the end of time
Cocooned and made to slumber
The beings that come from darkness
A resurrection passage
Awakes the armies under earth
I walk the open steps to answer

Abyssious voice leads me onward
A fate unknown by a future
A scepter raised of Hades elders

Return to NOD

Serve the shadows mountain peaks under the glass mirrored skies
Sing the psalms of the wailing winds, the entrance seer will provide
Stars reveal the tattered map, a land cursed of time
So speak the words of our challenger seeking the ultimate prize

Speaking the words of the sorcerer's tongue
No one can stop what's already begun
Follow the footsteps and unlock the door
The giant you face has awakened
Fear is invoked by your trembling hands, the foe is deadly and wise

A sight that's filled the eyes of mighty men, the very cost of their lives
Take the aim of the shimmering blade, the vulnerable spot is precise
Swift is the hand of the waking beast, crown of two worlds is the prize

Blood will spill on the warrior's feet, casting the enemy aside
Exalting the hero for evermore, steps to the throne of the eyes
Serve the shadows mountain peaks under the glass mirrored skies
Sing the psalms of the wailing winds, the entrance seer will provide

V

Snakes for the Divine

artwork by

Stash

Snakes for the Divine

Sinister Sister shall fall to the blade of my knife
Child of doom has begotten the power to rise
Sacrifice, morbid stories
Blood trickles down through histories

Given your sentence, you're handed the snakes of divine

Black as the devil, the night of the goat has arrived
All of the beaten the holding the sway and shall thrive
Fangs of the venomous reptiles

Suffering peace the endless time
Rise up, fall down
Gazing at gold, the ancient crime
Rise up, fall down
Cities come alive and they will die
Rise up, fall down
Ten thousand years are left behind
Rise up, rise up tonight

Given your sentence, you're handed the snakes of divine

Suffer the scourge by the powers invested in night
Running the course of the wolves and they're killing our kind
Oh, how their claws come ripping

Suffering peace, the endless time
Rise up, fall down
Gazing at gold, the ancient crime
Rise up, fall down
Cities come alive and they will die
Rise up, fall down
Ten thousand years are left behind
Rise up, rise up tonight

Blacked out sky, and beliefs in pillars time
Manifest death and our killers come to life
Breaking this spell and end my master's life

Repelled Repelled

Blacked out sky, and beliefs in pillars time
Manifest death and our killers come to life
Breaking this spell and end my master's life

Repelled Repelled

Blood trickles down through histories
Given your sentence, you're handed the snakes of divine
Blood trickles down through histories
Given your sentence, you're handed the snakes of divine

Frost Hammer

Dream being thrown down aloft between from the icy sky
Careful what to seek for inside the frozen mind
Permaglaze reflects this world distant to the thawed life
Frost clan blows the war horn without a fear or guise

Messiah of the glacian heir cold born to rise
Sullen boots impact upon deep the tundra ice
Glorify your greatness, sealed deal cold compromise
Catch the sun to melt these forborne galactic eyes

Plateau of Leng
Winter in veins
Hammers arise
To melt through the ice

Sail the seas of endless night
Despotic warlord casts his blight
Sons of the north abide

Frost child of abhorrent line
Feed the serpent, drink the wine
Granite heart, unrepentant

Frost hammer

Bastard Samurai

Count my fingers ten
Dressed to kill and think again
Count my fingers nine
Do the math your sacrifice
Son of a bitch should bleed awhile

Fighting under style
Sleeping under death awhile
Gladiators ring
Sharpening my blade to sting
Son of a bitch your fate I'll bring

Profit melee are all mesmerized All betray the bastard samurai
Profit melee on this killing floor All betray the bastard samurai

Bastard samurai

The killer I've become
Tattoo heart yakuza's thumb
Killing men aside
Severed heads abide
Son of a bitch should bleed awhile

Bastard samurai

Count my fingers ten
Dressed to kill and think again
Count my fingers nine

Ghost Neck

Feeding the needs of a desperate survival
Criminally active, not by choice
Overdosing on the mutual garbage
Skeleton the end unfolds
Empty raptured withered human
Cloaked dejection your demise
Shackled laid upon this dead prisoner
Screaming the waste, a deadly voice

Choke conjection and confusion
Surprised you're standing on your feet
Diabolic accusations
Pharisees are not to teach
Buy contempt and your conviction
Crushing others with disease
Horns are showing through the halo
Heroin is such a feast

Morning fever
Speaking in a vice
Dead deceiver
Sinking in the ice
Madman's sorrow
Oh i've seen things
You're nothing
Believe me

Running the circus like a leper
Licking your wounds, an injured hound
Fucked up, doomed and desecrated
Reside six feet underground
Mauled and incapacitated
Lame and dumb are at your feet
Never mind the true conception
Madman's sorrow is what you eat

Feeding the needs of a desperate survival
Criminally active, not by choice
Overdosing on the mutual garbage
Skeleton the end unfolds

Fire, Flood and Plague

The sanctioned annihilation
Death tax to the third world equation
The movement of the masses
Exodus of a populous
Breaking the sealed nightmare
Fire, flood, plague have come here
Mouth of the sword delivers
Spine, tendons, shakes and shivers

A light of basking lament
Father of manifestations
Mother of all creation
Gives doom to generations

Its bastard abomination
Humans with sickly faces
The soulless contradiction
A makeshift apparition
Lying in a pool of distance
Not knowing where the truth is
Standing in a graves museum
Lie down, and sleep this victim

A light of basking lament
Father of manifestations
Mother of all creation
Gives doom to generations

The fire hail raining
The storms torment destroying
Now come the angels threshing
Welcome to world extinction

We have been gathered here to
Die in this blackened nightmare
The psalm that separates us
Onto a pain in death

The place of Armageddon
Condemned and cursed the countdown
The terror of war and famine
The end of all we know is here

The sanctioned annihilation
Death tax to the third world equation
The movement of the masses
Exodus of a populous
Breaking the sealed nightmare
Fire, flood, plague have come here Mouth of the sword delivers
Spine, tendons, shakes and shivers

A light of basking lament
Father of manifestations
Mother of all creation
Gives doom to generations

How Dark We Pray

Serpent came to Eve from Tiamat
Immortality was known by man
Oh, how dark we pray

Spirit assassin dressed in black before your shrine
A woman's coffin sending shivers up my spine
Nailed are hands upon the cross so intertwined
A saintly mother sacrificed before your hive
They drink the life They eat of flesh
Oh, how dark we pray

The brain washed ghost of thought endless lies have come to bind
Four thousand years of mystery surrounding the signs
The Children scream aloud when pain and guilt align
The failing mass of contradiction in their finds
They drink the life They eat of flesh
Oh, how dark we pray

Shadows on the day of philstia
All will have to seek of Visigoth

The Serpent came to Even with a message from Tiamat
Death and immortality was known to man
Three had become four and five
Lilith had taken to conception
and was cursed to unearth where demons and man did not dwell together

Oh, how dark we pray

Holy Flames of the Fire Spitter

Deathly manner in the army to fight
Holy flames that have once come alive
We embrace tonight
Acrid sword, sharp as my life
Divine

Light the beacon through the embers of time
I've been betrayed, but now cross my line
Reborn to thrive
Cut 'em down, storming the hive
Divine

Fire Spitter
Fire Spitter

Power of the old ways shrined
Arise the spirit of the war god's kind
Fire baptized line
At your throat, accursed line

Fire Spitter
Fire Spitter

Deathly manner in the army to fight
Holy flames that have once come alive
We embrace tonight

VI

De Vermis Mysteriis

artwork by

Tim Lehi

Serums
of Liao

Priestess of a timeless cup, the taker has looked through old eyes
To see why of religion's course, my brothers path goes so wide
Killers maze, the holy's rage dreaded down under its size
Spirits tread, the lives gone dead, a risk to expose my face, my demise

Be thy eyes ancestors reign
Past attune and parafazed
Serum drunk reflect and chased
Bloodline trip enters their graves

In the winds of time blowing on
Of the hourglass Balteazeen

Drug of days, time malaise, shape taken enters the line
Ceremony ingest a poisonous fate know to time
Alchemy, black lotus ferment is carried afoot
Betwixt among relatives hiding a past that's a fold and aloof

Be thy eyes ancestors reign
Past attune and parafazed
Serum drunk reflect and chased
Bloodline trip enters their graves

In the winds of time blowing on
Of the hourglass Balteazeen

Bloody Knuckles

Knuckles thrash their way to find a skull that just can't hide
I duck and slip away to an uppercut and hide the feint
Lament and cry aloud as the opposition finds his deadly trap
Concuss the blow and find the targets places pinpoint, exact
Darkened goal reveal strength as my enemies see my war inside

Look defeat is chopping down to seek and death defile his demise Allude and cover up
anticipate the strike
Hardened punch deigns the vision of a face... and prize
The blood amongst this cage, the fiend within my rage
A ring of circumstance, heart is with me

Knuckles thrash their way to find a skull that just can't hide I duck and slid away to an
uppercut and hide the feint Lament and cry aloud as the opposition find his deadly trap
Concuss the blow and find the targets placed pinpoint, exact

The blood amongst this cage, the fiend within my rage
A ring of circumstance, devil with me

A puppets shadow dance, unkind the fall of chance
A prophet's mammon for your life
A cage of blood for your beaten size

The blood amongst this cage, the fiend within my rage
A ring of circumstance, devil with me

Fertile Green

Plant the seed, growing breed, within the turning weed, manifest oracles light
Harvest moon, Winter chills, strengthening breed that kills, fertile female gives sight
Sacrifice of males undone, slays to waste, what's been called unsung
Manifestia, green girl gives the way to follow, growing hollow

Smoke weed

Clone the creed, DNA, cutting back the trim delay, clouds of the spirit gave life
Earthen plant, fertile land, ready for the caravan, the girl of the world plants her plight
Stars agazing, microhazing, planet turned to climate phasing Face of beauty, conjures duty,
quest to find the green bud lurking

Kill me a sacrifice
A guidance given lights
Oracle ancient fire
Kill me a sacrifice
A Guidance given lights
Oracle ancient fire
Fertile green gives with pyre

Plant the seed, growing breed, within the turning weed, manifest oracles light
Harvest moon, winter chills, strengthening breed that kills, fertile female gives sight
Sacrifice of males undone, slays to waste, what's been called unsung
Manifestia, green girl gives the way to follow, grows mankind

Madness of an Architech

Black Stygian soil, conjures craft made undo times fertility
A karmic move you know the darkness always comes in threes
An alchemist finds frozen secret left behind the deeds
A wrath upon the humans less beyond this point society

Evolutions of a birth, a rhyme to tell this crimson tale
Evoke the faithful creed, the sacred secrets of society
Vanarian wars exploit the blood of
Stygian wise men, alchemy
Forgotten magic secrets shamed

Spiritual Rites

Ablaze with searing power
Sands of time will count the hours
Upside down turning faster
The come to burn the bastard
Read ethereal runes engraving
Appease the mass's craving
Heretic accused, a trial
Inquisition, last denial

I'll scourge your ghost
Salvation's tomb
Dark fanes my cloak
Deny my power and I'll burn you as the dead is

Demon knows your name this hour
Careful that it doesn't follow
Tiania elder bearing
Brings death amongst this hearing

I'll scourge your ghost
Salvation's tomb
Dark fanes my cloak
Deny my power and I'll burn you as the dead is

The wrath of priests are hollowed
Abominations followed
Awake to a death ancestor
Wrong the place to please the master
I'll scourge your ghost

Salvation's tomb
Dark fanes my cloak
Deny my power and I'll burn you as the dead is

King of Days

A psychopath has found a sight and a way to be the king of days
A rhyme without a poem and the luster of his last ways
The angels of death had a right and a cause for a sorrow to say
A mortal flight across a chasm and on to the underworld's graves

They sail a burning sun
A war they never won
They toss the fear aside
Never to ask for - pride

The spirits flights into a valley, a darkness that led them astray
An infant's eyes now open, with it a tempter, allude and betray
You know your master's leash is tight and keeps your death and your children at bay
The raging maniac aware and knows the cost of his earthly maze

They sail a burning sun
A war they never won
They toss the fear aside
Never to ask for — pride

De Vermis Mysteriis

De Vermis Mysteriis, awkward and curious, anoesis has opened its face
Kathulos, conjurer, tests of pain, Hasturers, pupils of black show their faith

Wizards, Hypoborea, craft of Khem, torn of the acriment write of their place
Winds of Zaar, origin traced, blue of skin, nuclear phase takes a race lost in time

Lance of kings, string of hate, obsessed upon morals and taint that obeys winds and kinds
Perpetrate, land affixed, Acheron escaping the scrolls and a fate of their shrine

Long live traveler
Winds now die
Dark place creature
Destined night

Romulus and Remus

Geminis suckled of the wolf
The milk that's drank will be withstood
Rome shall be
The royal blood in which we bask
An empire not seen in the past
Divinity

A way to carry on
Pack of the wild dogs
Belief that two are one
Blood in the sense so true

Death of the honor due
Festival of Mu
A way to carry on
Pack of the wild dogs

Land tides to raise the sunken span?
Atlantis sees a coming land
Rome shall be
Growth the dirt unto apore a plant
Adopt a populace who can't
Divinity

A way to carry on
Pack of the wild dogs
Belief that two are one
Brothers of the end the two
Death of the honor due

Warhorn

Bombarding its cavalry
Across the river they sleep
Bayonets running through the line
Cutting the men in half, divide
Muskets fire with powder
Weak willed men desert and cower
Hark, the sound of thunder
Waning the general's plunder

Leading the charge
Running them through
Soldiers death be true

Cannons fire as civil conflict
Bridles drenched blood crude
In this battle the screaming war
Cries that hear no truce
Charge on horseback breaks through the line
Grey and blue Death's truce
Hark the sound of thunder
Waning the general's plunder

Leading the charge
Running them through
Soldiers death be true

VII

Luminiferous

artwork by

Jordan Barlow

The
Black Plot

Pick a side cause the dogs come a begging
Best close your thighs cause the
Gods come a raping
Best hide your mind cause there's aliens mating
Truth is their lies less believed is their saying

Luminate phosphorus cells
Lust of an ethereal spell
Warlords of Hades are bound
Frequencies changing dark crowns

Reptilian eyes trick the arcane from under
Man's ancient pact darkness comes with the thunder
Poison gifts given death and asunder
We blame ourselves as the gods take their plunder

Luminate phosphorus cells
Lust of an ethereal spell
Warlords of Hades are bound
Frequencies changing dark crowns

Dark rites, seers given
Blood oaths, space time written
Dark rites, seers given
Can't stop what the Black Plot
Design has done

Carcosa

We have moved though time
Contemplate gold signs
Majik eyes a must
Dragons in the dust

Papalcy, the cult of existence
My demons run at resistance
Conjure life, inject the conjecture
Psychic anomaly catchers

The waking dreams align
Cross thread my rival's mind

Twin suns burn our fate
Collision worlds of great
Implore our earthly feet
In silent tragic means

Cosmic throne, earth and its citizens
To understand our existence
We have to dig and instruct the children
The beings of death that instilled them

The waking dreams align
Cross thread my rivals mind

Brain to flower of life
Waking up to time
Never have to die
Growing our third eyes

The Sunless Years

He's been taking the acid
And hooked into the light
Pondering radio fillings
And arcane satellites
Vampires take what they want of him
Visions to the nine
Keen, clean and wasting what may have been
Some people say something
Some people feel something

Black holes and time travel stratospheres
Visitors watching our binds
Wake up, there's gonna be hell to pay
Someone please tell them
This is our fucking lives
Chemtrails inhaled by infants
Overpopulate time
Killers made this political
Plaiedians hint at our minds

He shows insecure confidence
He's out of his mind
Sitting in black meditation
Someone please answer him
Someone please answer
He's been taking the acid
He's been taking the acid
He's been taking the acid
And arcane satellites

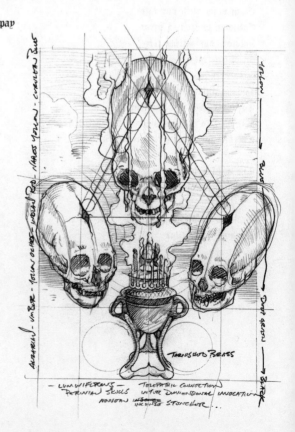

Slave the Hive

Reading your thoughts, just a bird in a cage, just a rat in a maze
Spiritual death, just a satanic catch, just a new god of lent
Dimensional screen, just a gospel to squeeze, just attention to seize
Plagerant muse, just a part for the fool, just a global epidemic

Flock of bats, unearthly addicts
Slave the hive, the clever bastards

Reading the lines just to pay your daily tides, just to bleed the vacant line
Web tainted minds, the majestic tribal sign, just inflicting mental crimes
Drawn to your grid, just a small reckless sin, just a life changing crypt
Gambit aflame, just to keep the cattle lame, your lobotomy is here

Flock of bats, unearthly addicts
Slave the hive, the clever bastards

They got us wired to the reptile brain, your life is not the same, this world is insane
Played by the man, just a torturous hand, executing his plans
Taunt you and tease, at the end of the chain, just accepting the game
Ever think twice in your evil device, how the programs concise
Digital tweak, the religion to seek, just a stab from the creeps

The Falconist

The great awakening and I don't feel better
Some of us take the pain
And the monsters are real
I could lie but its hunting us
As the fates draw nearer
We foresee the absolute
And the jackal is here

You can see me flying above the rift
Watch me diving, play the risks

I could see a long way off
Like a lighthouse keeper
The insane and the somber crowd
When doom whispers here
Hunter from a slight of wing
I'm a run kill catcher
Saw things from a hawk eye view
Falls a prophet of flight

You can see me flying above the rift
Watch me diving, play the risks
You can see me flying
Watch me diving
From the wrist, the Falconist

A kill to make the day
Got a monsters feather
Think your gonna take me down
I'll win this for real
Having been on the higher ground
And I shoot from the lever
I'm a bird of prey
And your kill in my eye

You can see me flying above the rift
Watch me diving, play the risks
You can see me flying
Watch me diving
From the wrist The Falconist

Hooded raptors
Bow from perch to Earth
Creance kept val chatri viced
Alright!

The great awakening and I don't feel better
Some of us take the pain
And the monsters are real

You can see me flying above the rift
Watch me diving, play the risks
You can see me flying
Watch me diving
From the wrist, the Falconist

We've lived a thousand years
And death had left alone
The assasian's fate is forged
On deeds of golden thrones

Dark Side of the Compass

A place where sunken ships never venture again
Sucked in by the vile catchers abyss
Panels and dials confuse on and off are amiss
Lost track can the voids return us to this

We can't find the direction of now
Compass and Earth are turned upside down

Appearance vastly fades from the radar screen blips
Cockpit askewed and caught in strange mist
Pilots or hope of life, ghost will never be found
Pay the price, missions sunk or just drown

Fleet ships and squadron aces disappear in the sound
Vorticies and portals mysteries found
On the way where the devil lay supernatural crowns
Graveyards, our dead will never be found

The Cave

Calm your heart and make it still
Take your time and get your fill
Dust moves on the floor
It's my head behind your door

We give our souls and find tomorrow
We laugh in death and kill the pain
Our sins and thoughts are left inside
Darkness the cave in which I hide

Work your art and do it well
Took the road to live in hell
The past is dead and now is now
Escape the reaper with our vow

We give our souls and find tomorrow
We laugh in death and kill the pain
Our sins and thoughts are cleansed inside
Darkness the cave in which I hide
Brother brother heal me, death has come to pray
Woman woman heal me, doom is where I lay

The blood haunts abandoned stone
We pour the wine to make it gone
Someone had to make a mess
Game of chess no pieces left

We give our souls and find tomorrow
We laugh in death and kill the pain
Our sins and thoughts are left inside
Darkness the cave in which I hide
Brother brother hear me
Watch the words you say
Father father hear me, doom is where I lay
Woman woman hear me, watch the words you say

Luminiferous

The paradigm of his last known crime
All the fingers point at you
Salutations fly from the dogmic eyes
As your judgment comes to view
Witness lies as you're charged with life
Sentenced death, so cold, so true
No choice you had, on this earth so sad
Find the strength to pull us through
Take the fall for a fate so tall
Retribution paid in full
Gavel strike, as the jury sighs
Unanimous and crude
Barrister with the white wig of fear
Unparoled time served accrued
666 and they got their list
And in time you'll see it's true

You know we never meant this
Serving luminiferous
Die to live amongst us
Serving luminiferous
Black the piranhas breathless
Serving luminiferous
Block the luminescence
Seeing luminiferous

Hammer, anvil, judge of torment
6 billion humans doomed
Luminiferous, souls of stardust
Reverence 432
Evolution virus, once inside us
Injection chip so new
If we relied on reptoid kindness
I think we're all just screwed

The Leathal Chamber

I magnetized, I realigned the terror force field view
It's solarized with wings of fire like giants cosmic do
A last chance ship ascends, our lives and hopes depend
The capsule holds surviving ghosts of sacred souls that flew
We travel back when time began to view the mythos true
Samsara change, caved mountain range, expose the race that knew

A last chance ship ascends, our lives and hopes depend on
A gift inspired, that made us slaves through mining gold and crude
The twin suns locked in cadence, vast magnetic pull
Nubiru speculation now confirming truth
A solar wind as time begins as man is birthed to new
A race of giants dimension spires to help them travel through
A last chance ship ascends, our lives and hope depend
Make cursed beings, galactic schemes, explaining overdue
The twin suns locked in cadence, vast magnetic pull
Nubiru speculation now confirming truth

I magnetized, I realigned the terror force field view
It solarized with winds of fire like giants cosmic do
A last chance ship ascends, our lives and hopes depend
The capsule holds surviving ghosts of sacred souls that flew
The twin suns locked in cadence, vast magnetic pull
Nubiru speculation now confirming truth

VIII

Electric
Messiah

artwork by

Derrick Snodgrass

Spewn from the Earth

Spewn from the earth
Deep in Terra's girth
Old ones from below, once the spell awakens
Comes the armies never known

Goliath now awakes
Fallen Babel's wraiths
Lost the golden age
Tramples at the temple, once the people are enslaved

Gone insane
Feel the ancient wrath
Gone Insane
Lords of pasts

Wicked kings prevail
Behemoth slumber failed
Loins of Annukiah, procreate the evil
As their beastly races thrive

Return the arcane throne
Of Gilgamesh's clone

King Og shatters the veils
Brings the whip of fire and will rape and copulate

Juggernauth
Kings to Copulate
Juggernauth
Giants seed
Buried in the mountains
Cryogenic lines

Rejuvenate the terror of old and scourge again with fire

Spewn from the earth
Deep in Terra's girth
Old ones from below, once the spell awakens
Comes the armies never known

Gone insane
Feel the ancient wrath
Gone Insane
Lords of pasts

Steps of the Ziggurat

Reckless abandon the overlords
The sigh of landing indigenous hordes
Plunder abundance demands the blackened swords
Genetic workers endure our earthen toil

Annunaki queen gives the doom of wombs
I take my place in the ranks of war
Deception from the first one born of the clay to live and die in scorn
From this clay we'll rise again with our fury stronger than before

Barbarian she rides the chrome time doors
The vault of Hades gives the golden plumes
The mines of gods, 200,000 years in the dark to be ignored
Revolt is brewing Iggigi looming, surrounds the house of the tyrant lord

Reckless abandon the overlords
The sigh of landing indigenous hordes
Plunder abundance demands the blackened swords
Genetic workers endure our earthen toil

House of Enlil

From the mountains
From the waters of the earth
I have heard the call Nineveh
From the forests
From the deserts of earth
I've become the son of war
From the darkness
From the heavens
From the furnace
From the darkness
From the heavens
From the furnace
From the masters
From the devils of old
We have sacrificed the bull
From the temples
From the platforms of Uhr
We remain the clashing gods

Electric Messiah

Stealing the blades from the old gods' grave
Thunder & firestorm
Tempting the wrath from the giant's path
Grip on the battle axe
My war has come to you
Usurp my throne & I'll sink my teeth in

Electric messiah
Thunder & fire
Electric messiah
Thunder & fire

Pack of hell from the devil's well
We take a drink or two
Sever the wrist & the blood is fixed
Worship the followless
My war has come to you
Usurp my throne & I'll sink my teeth in

Electric messiah
Thunder & fire
Electric messiah
Thunder & fire

All give praise as the ace hits the stage
All are amazed at the cards that he played
My homage paid to the king in his grave
He's playing bass & he's melting your face

All give praise as the ace hits the stage
All are amazed at the cards that he played

Sanctioned Annihilation

Hold on tight
We're in for a ride
Vigils of midnight terrorize the world at birth vaccinate the cured
All is drown in the waters of murk
The bomb explodes and scorches the earth
The plot to kill cleansing the state undone
Serpent of a thousand lies, beneath
Askew, disproved we're out of reach
A clinch in the mind of disbelief
Take what you will for its deceit
Hold on tight
We're in for a ride
The elite eye, the blind belief is lost and burn
The gavel down and all of this has lost its worth
The skeleton has made its secrets known
Dominant agendas through the black magic sewn
All is drown in the waters of murk
The bomb explodes and scorches the earth
The plot to kill cleansing the state
A clinch in the mind of disbelief
Take what you will for its deceit
Once we know the waker's will become
Once we understand it comes undone
Serpent of a thousand lies, beneath
Askew, disproved w're out of reach
A clinch in the mind of disbelief
Take what you will for its deceit
The sanctioned annihilation, prepare for devastation
Visual war perversion, death tax to the third world occasion
We see the thousands here to die
Thus proves a sad existence
Cast down the serpent devious, the deformed racist heretic
Mortar off the backs of carrion, a psalm that separates us
We see the thousands here to die
Thus proves a sad existence
A cast black swift of prudence, Among the elitists kill lists
Prejudice!

The Pallid Mask

On gallows high, where the blood flows the reddest
The noblest place to die is where we die the deadest
Deception your sin, the world will give in
Delusions of the cowards

I've seen Babylon, her fires burn so white
The whole world lay in Pandamine
We grasp our rifles tight

All is redeemed when the fates have been seen
The chronicles of miles

Here lies Babylon, it's come within the hour
Trumpets awake to warn the world
The milk of time has soured
Deception your sin, the world will give in
Delusion of the cowards

On gallows high, where the blood flows the reddest
The noblest place to die is where we die the deadest

I've seen Babylon, her fires burn so white
The whole world lay in Pandamine
We grasp our rifles tight

All is redeemed when the fates have been seen
The chronicles of miles

God of the Godless

Mannequin, imitation grin
Find a soul not left inside
Algorithmic, take my assistance
There's something there to hide
Why?

Androidic man, he sells what he can
While we're all just set to die
By your own hand, draw a line in the sand
Recreate a soulless life

Our creator, we don't fear you
Do your maker, we don't care who
You put me here to serve you
They put us here to help who?

Whoa, demutanize, now their line is cursed
Bring an end all left to fry
Speak not a word about the castrated herd
Being man is now a crime

The robotize, now we're finalized
Part of the mechanized decline
Total eviction, the situation fits you
Or a chosen time to rise

Our creator, we don't fear you
Do your maker, we don't care who
You put me here to serve you
They put us here to help who?

Stupid man, I'm chained and slaved to
Stupid man, my help will scourge you
Stupid man, I'm chained and slaved to
Stupid man, my help will scourge you

Freebooter

Open the seas to my plight
Winds in the gales of desire
Scourge of the port towns in sight
Cannons lay waste

And there's salt in our veins, giving death is our trade to the end
Skeletal flag and the fires that blaze seen for miles
Sword to the throat of the innocent
Black is our storm and you'll never escape our attack

The Crown and The Royals conspire
Sending the men

On a quest with Sir Drake to the cities to be played or sacked
No quarter to give, no prisoners will live past the hour
Sword to the throat of the innocent
Letter marquee for the crimes done at sea, crowns conspire

The corpse of the bastard is nigh
Brave men will kneel and die
The cowards and women will run
Murder and rape

And there's salt in our veins, giving death is our trade to the end
Skeletal flag and the fires that blaze seen for miles
Sword to the throat of the innocent
Black is our storm and you'll never escape our attack

Keelhauled and nailed to the mast
I've read the stars and crossed the leagues to bring you death
Death!

The Witch and the Christ

Roll the bones and dice
A pagan sacrificed
A fleeting state of mind
My hair begins to rise
Rise!

I pay my demon's price
The tree was shaken thrice
The spell was dealt the crone
The knuckle and the stone

The blood on my clothes
My family's demise
A cryptic wolf lunatic
The Witch and The Christ

She's traded the root of me
For carnivorous eyes
The baffling truth of it
The Witch and The Christ

The bloody pentecost
The true belief is lost
Lurker in darkest forests
The thirst for blood is quenched

Drowning Dog

The worship of inferae tombs
A communion of sycophants
How long is the line to our doom
Deceivers and lying chants

And goddamn you
You're the shadows of men
And goddamn you
For it's kill or be killed in the end

The numbers crossed lines in the sand
The pools of human rats
Their tails are twisted and tied
Eat of thy poison divine

And goddamn you
You're the shadows of men
And goddamn you
For it's kill or be killed in the end

And goddamn you
You're the shadows of men
And goddamn you
For it's kill or be killed in the end

The torturer slowly brought doom
Irreverent the ingrate laughed
Mendacious and full of black rants
Dark grins and knives in backs

And goddamn you
You're the shadows of men
And goddamn you
For it's kill or be killed in the end

Take what is given to you
Death surrounds you
Stuck low with souls for the moon
Death surrounds you
Black garbs, the hosting of two
Death surrounds you

Take what is given to you
Death surrounds you
Take what is given to you
Death surrounds you
Stuck low with souls for the moon
Death surrounds you

Death surrounds you